A Walkers' and Boaters' Guide to the Chesterfield Canal and Cuckoo Way

Christine Richardson and John Lower

The Hallamshire Press

A Richlow Guide

Copyright © 1994 Interleaf Productions Limited

Published by The Hallamshire Press
The Hallamshire Press is an imprint of
Interleaf Productions Limited
Exchange Works
Sidney Street
Sheffield S1 3QF
England

Typeset by Interleaf Productions
and
Printed in Great Britain
by
The Cromwell Press
Wiltshire

British Library Cataloguing in Publication Data

Richardson, Christine
  Walkers' and Boaters' Guide to the
  Chesterfield Canal: Richlow Guide
  I. Title   II. Lower, John
  914.25204
  ISBN 1-874718-25-3

Contents

Drakeholes

Introduction

This guide covers the 46 miles of the Chesterfield Canal between the River Trent and Chesterfield, via Retford and Worksop. The villages along the route are also included.

It contains practical information for canal users: towpath walkers, road visitors, anglers and boaters. Also included are interesting facts about what can be seen today, and the canal's history. A section on boat access via the River Trent can be found on page 74.

The authors are local enthusiasts who, over a number of years, have explored the canal by foot and by boat, and are regular contributors to national waterways magazines.

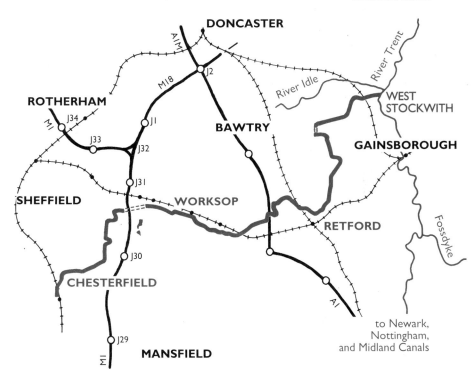

Brief Description

The Chesterfield Canal is one of the country's most pleasant waterways. Its 46 miles pass through open countryside in three counties: Derbyshire, South Yorkshire and Nottinghamshire.

It has 65 locks (59 narrow and 6 wide); two tunnels, Norwood (2,893 yards); and Drakeholes (154 yards); four reservoirs; and numerous bridges and aqueducts.

The 29 miles in Nottinghamshire pass through quiet countryside, all but three miles usable by pleasure boats between the River Trent and Worksop. This stretch gives a good impression of how the canals were before the waterways 'boom': no gift shops, peaceful, with plentiful wildlife and fish. The towpath is in very good condition throughout. It is also worth exploring the nearby villages, as a large part of the area's interest would otherwise be lost.

For the remaining 17 miles to Chesterfield the canal is in various states of disuse and restoration, and passes through changing scenery. Between Worksop and Kiveton Park the canal is again in remote countryside, with a good towpath, and includes the picturesque hamlet of Turnerwood; in the Rother Valley and Derbyshire the landscape is more scarred by past industrial use. However, it is on these sections that some of the most interesting features can be found: unique groups of (staircase) locks; Norwood Tunnel, the longest in the country when opened in 1775; and more and hillier countryside. Kiveton Park to Chesterfield may be walked throughout, with some detours, but the quality of the path cannot be guaranteed. The situation is constantly changing as various sections are currently being restored, including the towpath.

The towpath forms a long-distance walk called the 'Cuckoo Way', the name referring to the nickname once given to the canal's working boats by the Trent boatmen.

Navigation
The only access point for non-trailable boats is via the River Trent at West Stockwith. Trail-boats may use various slipways. Navigational information, for the canal and the River Trent, is on pages 75-77 and Maps 6-12 covering the navigable part of the canal.

Angling
Angling is very popular and the canal is a top-class coarse fishery. However, all the sections in water are controlled by various owners, clubs and associations. Details are on page 8.

Key to Maps

✝	Church	MS	Milestone (number = distance in miles from Chesterfield)
CP	Car Park		
FC	Fish and Chip Shop	RD	Refuse Disposal
G	Garage (fuel)	SS	Sanitary Station
GS	General Store	W	Water Point
LB	Letter Box	═	Towing path; canal navigable
MUS	Museum	≡	Unnavigable
PH	Public House	≣	Filled in
PO	Post Office	·····	Old line of canal or feeder stream
T	Telephone		Bridge
🚌	Bus		Aqueduct
🚆	Railway Station		Lock
- - -	Footpath		Staircase lock and number of chambers
— + —	Disused railway/cycle path/ bridleway		Turning point for 70ft craft
			Rivers, with direction of flow

Interesting Features to Look For along the Canal

Although the canal is now used for pleasure, many features of the days of the old horse-drawn working boats can still be seen.

Rope Grooves
The tow-rope between a horse and a boat was quite long. When a boat-horse emerged from under a bridge and regained the towpath, the boat was some way behind, and was still passing under the bridge. Therefore the tow-rope was at an angle and rubbed against the edge of the bridge and, many boats later, wore a groove in the brickwork. The best example is Lady Bridge (No. 54), but there are many others (see page 42).

Stop-Grooves
At some narrow points there are grooves in the stone or brickwork on both banks of the canal. If the canal is leaking, or a length has to be drained for maintenance work, then the required section can be dammed off by slotting planks into these grooves.

Milestones
These were placed along the canal because the canal company earned its money by charging boats a toll — a set amount per ton, per mile. Most of the original stones have been lost, but the Chesterfield Canal Society is gradually replacing them.

Winding Holes
This is the canal name for a turning place for boats. Boats can be up to 70 feet long, the length of the locks, and many cannot turn in the normal width of the canal. At winding holes the canal is widened to allow the longest craft to turn. They are marked on Maps 6-12 for today's boaters.

Turnover Bridges
The canal builders kept the towpath to one side of the canal whenever they could, but sometimes it had to change sides. Usually the bridges at such points were cleverly designed so that the boat-horse could cross to the other side without the tow-rope being untied.

Narrow and Wide Locks
To be commercially viable, working boats had to carry approximately 20 tons. If they were long rather than wide, a canal and its locks could be built narrow, and costs saved. Very early in the canal age, therefore, it was agreed that canals would be designed for such boats and the standard lock would be 7 feet wide and 72 feet long. However, canals near rivers often had wider locks so that large river boats could use them. The Chesterfield Canal has both types: narrow (7ft) between Chesterfield and Retford, and wide (15ft) between Retford and the River Trent.

Staircase Locks
Staircase locks are those built with two or more lock chambers adjacent, sharing the intervening gates.

Lock Houses
The only lock with a keeper is West Stockwith. However, the old keepers' houses still survive at some locks: for example, Osberton, Gringley, Forest, and Hollingwood.

British Waterways
Most of the navigable canals in Britain belong to the state-owned British Waterways. BW owns the stretch of this canal that runs from Norwood Tunnel to the River Trent. The rest of the canal has various owners — private individuals and local councils. Along the navigable section are BW facilities for boaters: mooring points above and below locks, as boats must stop to open the gates; and at strategic sites there are rubbish bins, toilet disposal points, and taps for filling drinking water tanks. Most are kept locked and crews open them with a special BW key. The easiest to see are at Clayworth and West Stockwith.

Further Information

Telephone Numbers

The digits in brackets to be omitted when dialling before 1st August 1994.

Chesterfield Canal Society

Tapton Lock Cottage, Lockoford Lane, Chesterfield, Derbyshire S41 7JB (registered office)

The Secretary, 18 Rosedale Avenue, Chesterfield S40 2UY
Tel: 0(1)246 559054

British Waterways

The Boatyard, Off Holmes Road, Lincoln LN1 1RF
Tel: 0(1)522 520148; also 0(1)636 704481

Inland Waterways Association

1 Vicarage Way, Arksey, Doncaster DN5 0TG
Tel: 0(1)302 873127

Derbyshire County Council Ranger Service

Tel: 0(1)246 866990

Head of Navigation Plaque

0(1)909 472791

Ramblers' Association

7 West Carr Road, Retford DN22 7NN
Tel: 0(1)777 700350

National Rivers Authority

Corringham Road, Gainsborough DN21 1QH
Tel: 0(1)427 612205

Tourist Information

Chesterfield	0(1)246 207777
Retford	0(1)777 860780
Rotherham	0(1)709 823611
Worksop	0(1)909 501148

All have free listings of accommodation in their canal area.

Boat Clubs

Retford & Worksop Boat Club, Clayworth Wharf, Clayworth, Retford
Tel: 0(1)777 817546

Retford Mariners' Boat Club, 6 Rose Avenue, Retford DN22 7HR
Tel: 0(1)777 702705

West Stockwith Yacht Club, The Yacht Basin, Canal Lane, West Stockwith, Misterton, Doncaster DN10 4ET. Tel: 0(1)427 890673

Trent Boating Association, 78 Old Retford Road, Sheffield S13 9RA

Angling Clubs/Societies

A permit is required on the canal, including the reservoirs. At the moment, angling is not allowed on the Derbyshire section.

Sheffield and District	0742 434740
(after 16th April 1995 will be	0114 243 4740)
Worksop and District	0(1)909 474940
Retford and District	0(1)777 701090
Worksop United	0(1)909 475369
Grafton Angling Society	0(1)909 474940

Public Transport

See page 18.

Maps

Ordnance Survey Landranger Series 1:50000

Sheets 119 (Chesterfield end), 120 (Staveley to Wiseton), 111 (Norwood to Retford), 112 (Clayworth to River Trent)

Ordnance Survey Pathfinder Series 1:25000

See canal map pages.

Further Reading

Richardson, Christine, *The Waterways Revolution: From the Peaks to the Trent* (1992; ISBN 1-85421-161-7). The building of the Chesterfield Canal.

Chesterfield Canal Society, *The Chesterfield Canal* (1991; ISBN 0-951346-01-9). Booklet, general guide and short history.

Roffey, James, *The Chesterfield Canal* (1989; ISBN 0-86023-461-4).

Hadfield, Charles, *The Canals of the East Midlands* (David & Charles, 1970; ISBN 7153-4871-X). History.

Bowskill, Derek, *Northeast Waterways* (Imray, Laurie, Norie & Wilson, 1986; ISBN 0-85288-099-5). Boating and navigation guide.

Nottinghamshire County Council, *The Trent Valley Way* (available from Dept. of Planning & Economic Development, Notts County Council, Fox Road, West Bridgford, Nottingham NG2 6BJ. Tel: 0[1]602 774483). Walking guide.

Public Houses

Key
Meals: L = Lunchtime; E = Evenings
Children: ✔ = Children welcome;
M = Children welcome when taking a meal

Bridge No.	Distance from Canal (yards)	Pub Name	Meals	Children	Beer Garden	B+B
2	300	The Lockoford Inn 0(1)246 275844	L/E	✔		✔
3		The Mill Tel: 0(1)246 273807		✔	✔	
10	1 mile	The Elm Tree Tel: 0(1)246 281606	L	✔	✔	
18	100	Sitwell Arms Tel: 0(1)246 435226	L/E	M		✔
27		Navigation Inn Tel: 0742 (0114 2) 485772	L	✔		
29		The Angel Inn Tel: 0742 (0114 2) 485607	L/E	✔	✔	
31	50	The Station Hotel Tel: 0(1)909 773201	L/E	✔	✔	
38		The Station Tel: 0(1)909 472244		✔	✔	
38	500	The Hewett Arms Tel: 0(1)909 500979	L/E	✔	✔	
40	50	The Woodhouse Inn Tel: 0(1)909 472747	L/E	✔	✔	
42		The Wharf Tel: 0(1)909 501600	L/E	✔	✔	
42		Canal Tavern Tel: 0(1)909 481965			✔	
51		The Chequers Tel: 0(1)777 703329	L/E	✔	✔	
Town Lock	150	The Albert Hotel Tel: 0(1)777 708694	L/E	✔		✔
Town Lock	100	The Clinton Arms 0(1)777 702703	L/E	✔	✔	
57		Packet Inn Tel: 0(1)777 706948				
59		Hop Pole Tel: 0(1)777 702409	L/E	M	✔	
62		The Gate Inn Tel: 0(1)777 703397	L/E		✔	
62	1 mile	The King's Arms 0(1)777 202930	L/E		✔	
66		The Boat Inn Tel: 0(1)777 700158	L/E	✔	✔	✔
67		The Brewer's Arms Tel: 0(1)777 816107	L/E	✔	✔	
67	250	The Blacksmith's Arms 0(1)777 818171	L/E	✔	✔	
73		The Griff Inn Tel: 0(1)777 817206	L/E	✔	✔	✔
74	1,000	Bluebell Inn Tel: 0(1)777 817406	L	✔	✔	
77	700	The Brickmaker's Arms Tel: 0(1)427 890375	L/E	M	✔	✔
84		The Packet Inn Tel: 0(1)427 890559	L/E	✔	✔	
85		The Waterfront Inn 0(1)427 891223	L/E	✔	✔	

History

Construction

The Chesterfield is one of this country's earliest canals. The planning started in 1768, in the wake of the successful Bridgewater Canal near Manchester. The original impetus came from the business community of Chesterfield, but at an early stage influential men in Retford offered their financial and political help — but only if the canal went via their town and Worksop, rather than the original route to Bawtry.

The goal was to link the inland towns with the River Trent, then one of the country's great trading highways.

The Principal Engineer was the nationally famous James Brindley, but he was involved in too many schemes to spend much time at any one of them. Therefore, day-to-day surveying and construction work was delegated to an assistant; on this canal it was John Varley.

Construction work started at Norwood in the autumn of 1771. It was to be a tremendous feat of engineering for the time. The 2,893-yard Norwood Tunnel was, at the time of its completion in 1775, the country's longest. It is also probable that the locks near Thorpe Salvin were the first to be built as a multi-staircase flight. And there is evidence that Norwood Locks originally contained a six-rise staircase; if so it would be the only such configuration ever built in England. The initial progress was eastwards towards the Trent; the Derbyshire section was done later.

Work was completed in 1777, and on the 4th of June the official opening ceremony was held at Tapton Lock, Chesterfield.

● For details of the construction of the Chesterfield Canal see:
Christine Richardson, *The Waterways Revolution: From the Peaks to the Trent, 1768–1778* (1992; ISBN 1-85421-161-7).

The Trading Years

For the first ten years financial returns were diminished by interest payments on the loans required to complete construction. But in 1789 the first dividend was paid, and the canal continued to be moderately prosperous until the middle of the 19th century. The major cargo was coal, but stone, corn, lime, lead, timber and iron were carried, as well as various sundry items. The most illustrious cargo was the stone to rebuild the Houses of Parliament after the great fire of 1834. The quarry was in North Anston, and during the

1840s the stone was loaded at Kiveton Park and carried to West Stockwith for onward shipping to Westminster by Trent sloops.

The Railway Years

As on most canals, the railways heralded the end of profitable trading. The canal company tried to alleviate the impact by forming its own railway in 1845, the Manchester & Lincoln Union. However, numerous mergers resulted in the Manchester, Sheffield & Lincoln Railway (MSLR) taking over the canal in 1847. In 1890–91 several canal diversions were made because of the building of branches of the MSLR.

Decline

By 1905 the tonnage carried on the canal had lessened considerably, and only 40 working boats remained. Norwood Tunnel had always given trouble: the coal seams in the area caused subsidence and maintenance costs were high. Finally, on the 18th of October 1907, the tunnel roof collapsed again and the MSLR decided it could no longer justify the expense of re-opening the tunnel. The Chesterfield end of the canal was then cut off from the Trent.

Some trade continued, especially coal from Shireoaks and bricks from Walkeringham. By the late 1950s the only cargo being carried was probably warp from West Stockwith to Walkeringham: warp was a fine silt dredged from the Trent, dried, filtered and used for polishing metal in Sheffield's cutlery trade.

Restoration

The 1950s saw a growing awareness of the canals as a source of leisure. Vigorous campaigning by the Retford & Worksop Boat Club in the 1960s kept the canal in the headlines, and the 1968 Transport Act finally designated the 26 miles from West Stockwith to Worksop as a cruiseway for leisure use. Kiveton Park to Worksop was kept as a water supply route for the navigable section. To the west of Norwood Tunnel, infilling was proposed as far as Spinkhill, with the rest kept for supplying water to the works at Staveley and Renishaw. By 1976 it was felt that restoration beyond Worksop was desirable, and the Chesterfield Canal Society was formed to achieve that aim.

In the 1990s considerable restoration work has been done by the Canal Society and other groups, especially the five miles and five locks between Chesterfield and Staveley, but also at Renishaw, Shireoaks and Worksop. Good progress continues towards the complete restoration of the Chesterfield Canal.

The Boats of the Chesterfield Canal
The boats were not like the gaily painted vessels seen elsewhere on the canal system. They were basic working boats, and at no time were they painted with 'roses and castles', nor bedecked with lace plates or Measham teapots. Most of them were built in West Stockwith basin and their design was therefore greatly influenced by the River Trent craft that had been built in the village for centuries. They ventured out onto the Trent and carried the basic equipment needed on

the tideway: sometimes a mast and sail, usually some oars, always a long heavy chain for dragging along the river bed to give the boatmen some control of the boat.

The boats had cabins, but the entrances were flush to the deck. A typical working boat would have an aft cabin 4 feet 3 inches high, 9 feet long, and 6 feet 6 inches wide.

No complete Chesterfield Canal narrowboat has survived. The Boat Museum at Ellesmere Port has a bow section and hopes to replace the original front decking for future display.

Throughout the canal's history all working boats were horse-drawn.

An illustration of a working boat can be seen on the inside front cover.

Bridge weight-restriction sign

Wildlife

The canal is an important and rich habitat for wildlife. A wide variety of birds, animals and plants can be seen because the water, the water's edge, the canal bank and neighbouring fields all form different environments.

The canal is also a freshwater habitat, totally different from rivers: the water is slow-moving and of moderate depth, it has a greater range of daily and annual temperatures, and the bottom deposits are relatively undisturbed.

The following is a general guide to what may be seen and where. Further information can be found in specialist books on each subject.

Birds

Below are listed some of the birds that can be seen along the canal.

Blackcap

Beautiful loud, rich, pure warbling song heard in copses. Regarded by many as equal to the nightingale.

Bunting, Reed

Has a particular liking for canals and is often seen in the spring, singing perched on top of hedges, bushes or reeds.

Coot

Large black birds usually seen swimming on the canal, but also grazing on grasslands. Can be identified by the distinctive white patch that covers the front of the head and top of the bill: the reason for the saying 'bald as a coot'. The downy chicks have a red face and bill and, if seen apart from an adult, may be taken for moorhen young. Noisy splashy fights may occur when bordering territories meet. When hastily retreating, coots perform a mixture of running and flying across the surface of the water.

Cormorant

In the winter, widespread on estuaries and nearby inland waters; often seen in Stockwith basin. They spend much time perched on man-made structures. They dive for fish: eels are their favourite food.

Curlew

With a distinctive curved bill, these may be seen in the canal-side fields between Clayworth and Hayton.

Dabchick

Found on quieter stretches in winter, dabchicks are small, dumpy birds that dive at the first sign of danger. They feed by diving to catch small fish, mainly sticklebacks.

Fieldfare

A winter visitor often in mixed flocks with the redwing; it feeds on haws and other berries.

Goldcrest

In winter, it feeds in large mature canal-side gardens. It also joins flocks of tits. Often seen on King's Park stretch in Retford.

Golden Plover

Seen in large winter flocks in nearby fields with lapwings.

Harrier, Marsh and Hen

Rare, but seen at the end of the canal near the Trent.

Heron

Visible all times of the year, these are the largest wild birds that can commonly be seen. Most are active dusk and dawn, stalking slowly after fish, frogs, voles, insects, and eels. During the day they often stand motionless near the water's edge. They usually flap away at the last minute when disturbed. In flight the heron's size, long legs and bent neck make it unmistakable. May also be seen in fields, and herons nest in tall trees from February onwards. So silent by the water, but aggressive and noisy at the nest.

Kestrel

A common sight hovering over the canal bank or fields.

Kingfisher

Kingfishers are Britain's most exotic-looking birds. Always exciting to see, usually as an eye-catching bright flash of intense blue, flying at up to 25mph low to the water surface, wings rapidly whirring. When watching motionless for small fish from a branch over the water, they are surprisingly difficult to see. An old saying is 'only the righteous ever see a kingfisher'; if you think you qualify, good places to look are near Dixon Lock (No. 4), Thorpe Bridge (No. 32), Greenmile Bridge (No. 52), Taylor's Bridge (No. 71), and in the cutting north of Drakeholes Tunnel. In a frozen winter, kingfishers migrate to the coast using the canal and the Trent to navigate.

Coot

Kingfisher

Cormorant

Curlew

13

Heron

Swift

Barn Owl

Lapwing

Lapwing

In autumn and winter they mass in nearby pastures and ploughed fields. Also known as the peewit, from the call.

Moorhen

Black birds, often seen swimming on the canal. Smaller and more timid than coots, the red bill and front of head are the most obvious distinguishing marks. Thought of as water birds, they are nevertheless very adaptable and are able to climb trees, walk or run on flat ground, swim, wade or clamber through undergrowth. One of the few British birds that can swim well without webbed feet. They feed in fields as well as on the canal. From April to July the nests are conspicuous floating mats of dried vegetation, close to the water's edge. Nestlings swim almost at once: little fluffy, unsinkable specks that hide in the canal-side foliage when disturbed.

Owls, Barn

These hunt during the day and at dusk, and can be seen over the cricket pitch at Worksop, and between Wiseton and Clarborough. Others owls heard at night.

Partridge and Pheasant

Common in nearby fields.

Redshank

Often seen on passage in the spring; occasionally breeds alongside the canal.

Rook

All year; large noisy colonies in the tops of trees.

Sand Martin

The first of the swallow family to arrive; browner than the House Martin and lacking the white rump. They used to breed at Sandhill Lake in Worksop, and may still be seen gathering there in March and April.

Sandpiper, Common

Often seen on passage in the spring.

Shoveler

Less frequent than other ducks, but they have bred on the Osberton Estate.

Siskin

Winter visitors can be seen feeding in alder trees in King's Park in Retford.

Snipe

Occasionally breeds alongside the canal.

Sparrowhawk

Likes woodland or farmland — a favourite hunting site is the blackthorn scrub bordering the canal at Manton, near Worksop. Also seen between Drakeholes and Hayton.

Spotted Flycatcher

The Spotted Flycatcher arrives in late spring or summer. It darts out for flying insects from overhanging branches or dead trees. It can also seen in canal-side gardens at Retford.

Swallow

Regular summer visitors. They catch insects by the water: an abundant food source, especially when stirred up by a passing boat. The swallows swoop low, sometimes missing the crew by inches. Drakeholes is a good area to see them.

Swift

Summer visitors. They feed over the canal, and are common in and around the Nottinghamshire villages and Retford.

Tern, Common

Summer visitors anywhere along the canal, seen regularly along the Trent. Arctic Terns are seen occasionally in spring or autumn on migration.

Wagtail, Pied

Black and white, the female greyer. It catches insects by sudden dashes on the ground or bursts of flight. Likes feeding at lock by-washes.

Wagtail, Yellow

Three or four pairs nest between Worksop and Retford, and are often seen at Misterton. They feed at lock by-washes.

Warbler, Sedge

Arrives late April or May, and sings a noisy chattering song from low in canal-side reeds.

Water Rail

Unusual winter visitors, they like quiet reedy backwaters. More likely heard than seen, they have a very strange call uttered early or late in the day, sounding like grunts and squeals of a pig.

Wheatear

Seen passing on spring migration, especially on pastures or stony arable land between Retford and Lady Bridge (No. 54).

Mammals

Rabbits, hares, foxes, squirrels, are all seen in the fields or trees alongside the canal.

Stoats and *weasels* use the hedges by the towpath as hunting grounds.

Water voles. Small, brown, and furry, they are active during the day and often seen feeding on waterside plants. Usually the first sign is the ripples made as they swim across the canal. Make holes and tunnels in the banks, often with the entrance underwater.

Smooth newts. Four inches long, they spend most of their life on land, but never go far from water. The breeding season is from February to summer. They hibernate in damp, dark, well-concealed places.

Frogs. For much of the year they remain hidden in damp, dense, vegetation close to the canal. Most easily seen during breeding season which may start as early as February when they return to the canal in large numbers.

Bats. Can be found near Drakeholes tunnel and at Misterton. They spend the day in out-buildings, rock-fissures, hollow trees, or entrances to tunnels. They usually emerge soon after sunset, and often squeak in flight.

Insects

Damsel Flies are abundant June and July. Vivid-blue males can be seen resting on foliage in sheltered spots, flying over the water, or clinging to a floating leaf to support a greenish female as she submerges to lay her eggs.

Butterflies, such as orange-tip, peacock, red admiral, small tortoiseshell.

Pond Skaters appear to walk on the water. **Whirligig beetles** circle endlessly on the surface, especially where the water is clear and dappled by overhanging trees. **Water Boatmen** use paddle-shaped legs to propel themselves upside down through the water.

Shellfish

There are more than three dozen kinds of shellfish in the canal: from ten-inch *mussels* to tiny *valve snails*.

Plants

The canal and surroundings support over 200 types of flowering plants, most of which are best seen between June and September. Some like damp near the water, others have their roots in the water's edge, and many settle for half-way depth. Such is the variety that it is not possible to list them here.

    Meadowsweet is conspicuous on the damp soil of upper banks and towpath sides: tall-stemmed with large heads of fragrant creamy-white flowers in late July and August. The purple-flowered **Great Hairy Willow-Herb** can be seen, and the **Great Water Dock**. Among grasses and rushes, beware of: *Bitter-Sweet,* with purple flowers like those of potato and poisonous red berries; and the poisonous

Fool's Watercress, which looks like watercress but isn't. In the canal, *Flowering Rust* is tall with prominent pink flowers; *Arrow-Head* has white flowers. *Yellow Flag Iris* is a striking plant of the water edge, flowering from June to August.

Fungi

Please remember that some fungi are poisonous. The types listed grow in association with plants on the bank or towpath and are mainly seen in the autumn.

On trees. The Oak may have *Beef-Steak* fungus: like a juicy steak projecting from the trunk. Willow frequently has *Blushing-Bracket;* the pores on the underside bruise reddish when touched and give it its name. On ash, *King Alfred's Cakes:* hemi-spherical, black, and look like small burnt buns. On elder, frequently found is *Jew's-Ear* fungus, which looks and feels like human ears projecting from the wood. Around the base of trees, *Old Honey* fungus produces dense clusters of toadstools: honey-brown with dark-brown scales, a ring round the stem. Dead trees have a large number of various types: another *Honey* fungus spreads from one dead stump to another, producing dark brown strands, which look like old-fashioned leather bootlaces. *Lawyer's-Wig* or *Shaggy-Ink-Cap* has a shaggy surface like a barrister's courtroom wig, found on the towpath where roots or timbers are below.

Fish

With the exception of eels, these fish prefer the slow-flowing waters provided by the canal.

Bream

A shy fish that forms large shoals and frequents deep water in the winter. A deep body with a brown back, yellowish-brown sides, and brown fins. Average 9–16 ins.

Carp

Prefers weedy areas, and forms small shoals. Usually swims near the bottom, but on warm summer days will often bask lazily near the surface. Greenish-brown back, yellowish-brown sides, and small barbels at each side of mouth. Females grow to 9–19 ins.

Chub

The young form shoals, but older fish are solitary. Dark grey-green back, greenish sides, and red lower fins. About 16 ins. Feeds on other fish as well as plants and insects.

Eels

Lives in any type of water: still, flowing, fresh, or salt. Travels overland at night in wet conditions, so found in closed ponds and canals. They spawn in the Sargasso Sea, and stay in fresh water for up to twenty years. The females grow to 20–30 ins. Found all over the UK.

Perch

The most abundant European fish. Often forms large shoals, and is slow-moving. Brownish-green back with dark bars across it, yellow-green sides, and red lower fins. 8–11 ins.

Pike

The 'freshwater shark', feeding on other fish, young water-birds, and frogs. May live for twenty years, the females growing to 15–40 ins. Grey-green or brownish back, green sides with yellow spots or stripes, large teeth.

Roach

Member of the carp family. Feeds on small water insects and aquatic plants, mainly on the bottom. A dark rounded back, silvery-white sides, reddish eyes, and red fins. Average 5–10 ins.

Tench

Fond of water overgrown with vegetation, generally stays close to the bottom. A sturdy fish, with small eyes, brown-green back, sides with a golden sheen, and small barbels at both corners of mouth. Average 8–11 ins.

Public Transport

As public transport services can change at any time, it was not thought wise to include specific routes and times; instead, telephone numbers for the latest information have been included.

Rail
Main railway stations in the area are Sheffield, Doncaster and Gainsborough. Buses to the canal operate from these stations.
Along the canal there are stations at Chesterfield, Kiveton Park, Shireoaks, Worksop and Retford.

Information: Doncaster 0(1)302 340222;
Sheffield 0742 (0114 2) 726411;
Newark 0(1)636 704491

● **The station at Kiveton Park is canal-side at Dog Kennel Bridge (see Map 4), and a popular option is to walk from here to either Shireoaks or Worksop and catch the train back.**

Buses
The canal is well served by various bus companies, making it possible to walk many lengths and use public transport to return. Some people eventually walk the whole canal in such a way. The quiet countryside at the Nottinghamshire end is very popular for such visits, and that county's bus information service is centralised for ease of reference (see below).

Derbyshire
There is county-wide bus information on 0(1)246 250450, but individual operators are as follows:

Chesterfield Transport (0[1]246 207103) for Chesterfield, Brimington and Staveley

East Midlands Motor Services (0[1]246 211007) for Chesterfield, Staveley, Renishaw, Killamarsh, Shireoaks, Rhodesia and Worksop

Nottinghamshire
● **The county operates a very useful bus information hotline covering all service operators, including 'The Sherwood Forester'. The number for the canal areas is Retford (0[1]777) 710550.**

Locations on, or near, the canal that have a bus service are: Worksop, Ranby, Retford, Clarborough, Hayton, Clayworth, Wiseton, Drakeholes, Everton, Gringley-on-the-Hill, Misterton and West Stockwith.
   At the time of writing, the most useful services to enquire about are: 42, 95/96, 97, 98 and 100, all of which call at various canal locations. There are other services, however, including those to the canal from major rail stations.
   In summer months, Nottinghamshire also operates 'The Sherwood Forester', a popular bus network concentrating on leisure attractions, and using all-day 'ranger' tickets. A useful booklet and timetable is available from Tourist Information in Worksop and Retford (see page 8).

● *Telephone numbers: the digits in brackets to be omited when dialling before 1st August 1994.*

Bus painted with the canal's route

Chesterfield

Chesterfield, on the edge of the Peak District National Park, grew up around its famous open-air market. It was always a trading town, taking advantage of being at the hub of trade routes from all points of the compass.

Today the **Market Place** is still the heart of Chesterfield, and more than 200 stalls crowd into the area on market days — Monday, Friday and Saturday. Special markets are also held on most summer bank holidays. On the eastern side are the narrow streets of **The Shambles**, and the half-timbered **Royal Oak**, the town's oldest pub. On the southern side is the **Peacock Centre**, dating from 1500 and now housing the Tourist Information Centre.

However, the most famous feature of Chesterfield is undeniably the **Crooked Spire** of St Mary's church, which dominates the skyline on all approach routes to the town. It rises 228 feet, and twists and leans 9 feet 4 inches from its true centre. The reason? The fables are many, the facts few. The likely answer is that it was built with green unseasoned wood that has warped under the heavy lead covering. It was already distorted when the canal was built in the 1770s.

Spacious **Queen's Park** is a peaceful area with a lake. It is also a county cricket ground and Derbyshire play here several times during each season.

Chesterfield Museum has exhibits related to the canal and its place in the town's history. Just outside the town centre is the **Revolution House** — here local noblemen met to plan their influential part in the overthrow of King James II in 1688. It is now a museum; admission is free.

Tapton House was the home of George Stephenson the railway pioneer; he died here in 1848.

Chesterfield is also surrounded by many **interesting places to visit**: Chatsworth House, The National Tramway Museum, Blue John Caverns, cable-car rides at the Heights of Abraham, Haddon Hall, Bolsover Castle, and the beautiful Peak District National Park.

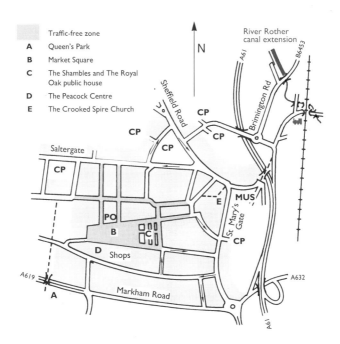

	Traffic-free zone
A	Queen's Park
B	Market Square
C	The Shambles and The Royal Oak public house
D	The Peacock Centre
E	The Crooked Spire Church

Map 1: *Chesterfield*

3.5 miles (OS Pathfinder, Sheets 761 and 762)

Navigation
As lengths are restored, details can be obtained from Derbyshire County Council, Ranger Service (see page 8).

Hollingwood Lock (No. 5)
Hollingwood Lock was built in the late 19th century when the new railway cut off the original line of the canal where it looped through Staveley Works. It was re-opened in June 1993.

Dixon Lock (No. 4)
The half mile above the lock was restored after open-cast mining had destroyed the original lock. A new lock is being constructed by the Canal Society, on a site 200 yards below the original.

Bluebank Lock (No. 3)
This lock has been restored by the Canal Society with financial assistance from British Coal.

Wheeldon Mill Lock (No. 2)
The length between the lock and Station Road has been restored using original stone and brick whenever possible. South of Station Road, Brimington Wharf has been cleared and old mooring rings are on top of the far bank stonework.

The Canal Society's Trip-Boat,
John Varley
The boat operates on the restored sections and may be seen moored in mid-stream (trip details can be obtained from the Chesterfield Canal Society). The boat is named after the Resident Engineer, an assistant of James Brindley who built the canal in the 1770s.

Tapton Lock (No. 1)
Tapton Lock was the first to be restored, in 1990. The towpath goes under the bridge. The canal's official opening was celebrated here on the 4th of June 1777 by a large crowd of people, including the Mayor of Chesterfield. The first boatload of cargo arrived, was raised in the lock, and pulled towards the town. Bands played there, and a feast was enjoyed by many, including nearly 300 navvies who were no trouble at all. On the 29th of April 1990, another crowd gathered, again including the Mayor of Chesterfield, and the first boats were raised in the newly restored lock. The lockhouse was built in the 1960s to replace an earlier one. The by-wash, taking away surplus water, can be seen by the top gate and runs underneath the house to below the bridge.

There are a number of plaques and memorials: three on the brickwork outside the bottom gates, and one on the far side of the top gate in memory of Trevor Dodds, a Canal Society volunteer who helped to restore the lock.

Tapton Tunnel
This is a new bypass built in the late 1980s. Strenuous efforts by the Canal Society resulted in the canal being provided with a navigable tunnel.

Tapton Mill Bridge
Chesterfield's famous 'crooked spire' church can be seen beyond the bridge. The towpath changes sides. The canal takes its initial water supply from the River Rother here, and a flood-gate protects the canal.

River Rother/Canal Junction
This is the western end of the Chesterfield Canal. The Rother drops over a weir on its way to join the River Don at Rotherham. Originally, the canal was to cross over the river and continue towards Chesterfield. Lack of funds meant a cheaper option was needed, although the canal company had no legal right to do so. The river was used to approach the town, thereby saving the expense of digging more canal.

Original Basin and Warehouse
This was built in the late 1770s so that boats could be unloaded off the river and cargoes stored. Little trace now exists, except the name of the adjacent Wharf Lane. The site is on the west of the river where the towpath changes sides. A path leads to a bridge over the Inner Relief Road, built on the line of the railway (Manchester, Sheffield & Lincoln line) that isolated the basin about 1890.

Later Canal Basin
This replaced the original when the railway was built. A small landing stage is on the entrance brickwork, alongside Holbeck Close. Not much can be seen now.

Towpath End
Access is from Holbeck Close, a cul-de-sac off Brimington Road (B6453), near the Trebor factory. The path is alongside the river.

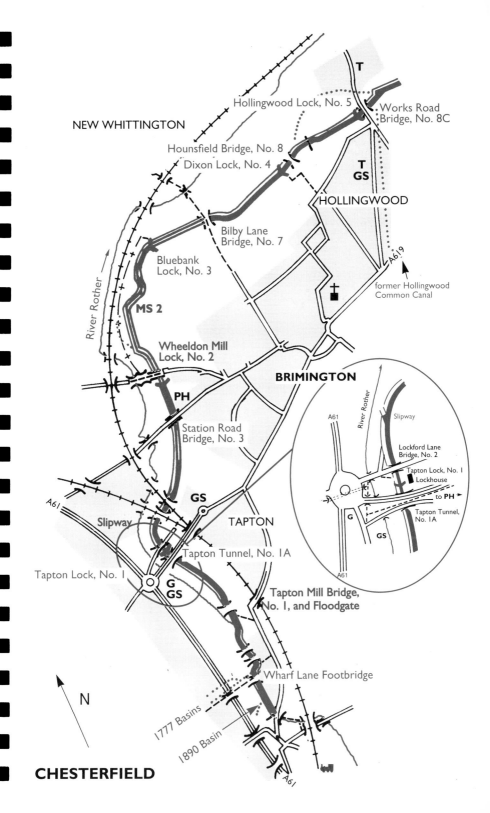

NEW WHITTINGTON

Hollingwood Lock, No. 5

T

Works Road
Bridge, No. 8C

Hounsfield Bridge, No. 8
Dixon Lock, No. 4

T
GS

HOLLINGWOOD

Bilby Lane
Bridge, No. 7

Bluebank
Lock, No. 3

River Rother

MS 2

A619

former Hollingwood
Common Canal

Wheeldon Mill
Lock, No. 2

BRIMINGTON

PH

Station Road
Bridge, No. 3

GS

TAPTON

Slipway

Tapton Tunnel, No. IA

Tapton Lock, No. 1

A61

G
GS

Tapton Mill Bridge,
No. I, and Floodgate

Wharf Lane Footbridge

N

1777 Basins

1890 Basin

CHESTERFIELD

A61

Inset:

A61

River Rother

Slipway

Lockford Lane
Bridge, No. 2

Tapton Lock, No. I
Lockhouse

to PH

Tapton Tunnel,
No. IA

G

GS

A61

The Chesterfield Canal Society
A Registered charity with over 600 members

Formed in 1976 the CCS campaigned tirelessly to raise awareness of the Chesterfield Canal and to demonstrate the benefits of restoration.

The Society is involved in:
- Practical restoration work
- Trip-boats
- Canal days
- Sales, exhibitions and slide shows
- Fund-raising
- Producing printed information
- School visits

Further information is available from:
Chesterfield Canal Society,
Tapton Lock Cottage,
Lockoford Lane,
Chesterfield S41 7JB

Or telephone the secretary on 0246 559054

John Lower's boat, Schandelle — the first vessel through the restored flood lock at Tapton, Chesterfield, 6th November 1993

Tapton Lock (No. 1) re-opening ceremony on 29th April 1990. The boat party includes the Mayor of Chesterfield, the town's MP (Tony Benn), and the Chairman of the Canal Society.

Canal Society members restoring Tapton Lock (No. 1)

Map 2: *Staveley*

4 miles (OS Pathfinder, Sheet 762)

Renishaw

Restoration here is the work of the Renishaw Environmental Action Group, aided by the Chesterfield Canal Society. Bridge 18 was rebuilt in 1993, and to the south the canal was straightened in 1890–91 to allow the building of the railway. The railway itself has now been converted into a path linking Staveley and the Rother Valley Country Park. Between Bridge 17 and Bridge 10 the course of the canal is infilled, and sometimes marked by little more than a public footpath through the fields.

Norbriggs Cutting

A branch of the canal built to link with the Chesterfield–Worksop turnpike road, now the A619. It also met a tramway to a colliery leased by the canal company, and a feeder bringing water supplies from the River Doe Lea.

Staveley Puddlebank

A high embankment carrying the canal over the River Doe Lea. This was a tremendous achievement by the canal builders, and may have been the last part to be completed in 1777. Footbridges pass over two places where the embankment has been breached.

Staveley

The town has a long history, and was mentioned in the Domesday survey of 1086. It was part of the estate of the Frecheville family in the 1500s, and later the property of the Dukes of Devonshire. The past two centuries have brought considerable industrial development: the nearby River Rother used to be the site of mills and a large ironworks, and in 1864 there were five collieries and 2,000 miners in the town. By the canal now is the Rhône-Poulenc chemical and pharmaceutical plant. However, Staveley is interesting and a good 'Town Trail' leaflet is available from Chesterfield Tourist Information.

To the south of Bridge 10, the canal has been dredged by the Chesterfield Canal Society, with the help of local contractors Fitzwise Limited.

Staveley Works

The bend in the canal 200 yards below Hollingwood Lock is where the original line looped through the Works (see Map 1). There was an iron foundry here on the River Rother from very early times. Eventually it grew into a massive complex with the old line of the canal through the middle of it.

Hollingwood Common Canal Tunnel
(See also Map 1)

The entrance can be seen on the far side of the canal: a small grille over an opening into the hillside. It was an underground canal leading to various coal seams along which boats carried coal from the working areas to the main canal. The boats were 21 feet long and carried the coal in seven tubs. The tubs were hoisted by crane and emptied into the boats on the main canal. In its working days, the tunnel was 6 feet high, 5 feet 9 inches wide, with a water depth of 2 feet, and just under 2 miles long.

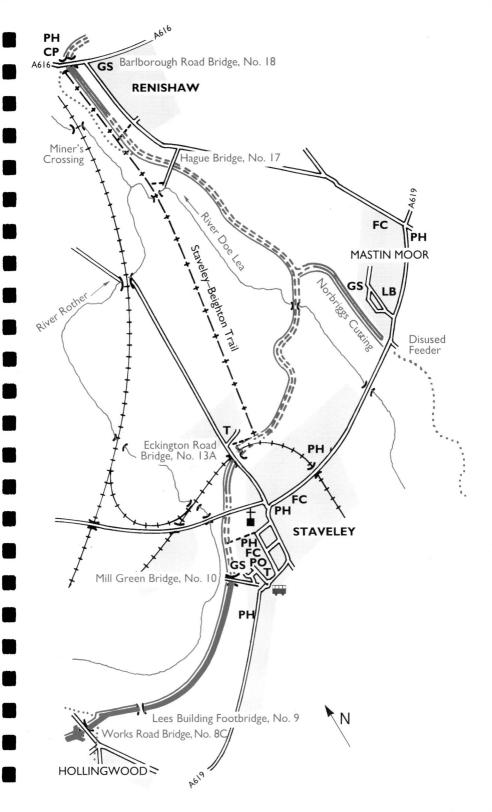

Breaking the concrete capping on Hollingwood Lock (No. 5) prior to restoration

Dredging the previously infilled canal at Chesterfield, between Tapton Lock (No.1) and Tapton Mill Bridge (No.1). This section was re-opened in Feburary 1994.

Map 3: *Killamarsh*

5 miles (OS Pathfinder, Sheet 744)

The towpath at Norwood is a public right of way, but is on private property. Please respect the owner's privacy.

Norwood Tunnel
This tunnel is 2,893 yards long. The bricked-up western portal is a few yards from the top lock. By the entrance, on the left when facing the tunnel, the ruins of the tunnel-keeper's cottage can be found in the undergrowth.

The construction of the canal started here in the autumn of 1771. It was also the site of the tunnel's official opening ceremony on the 9th of May 1775, at which people dressed in their finery — shareholders, engineers, and landowners; speeches were made and a band played. Then they boarded boats and went through the tunnel, with the band still playing!

Norwood Locks (Nos. 7–19)
Thirteen locks are situated within a third of a mile. They form a unique flight of four groups of 'staircase' locks (see page 7), and their 1775 construction date means they are a very early example of such locks. Between the top two groups is an old water-powered sawmill, now a private house. The large areas of water are side-ponds, storage areas for the large amount of water needed to operate staircase locks. These were filled from the reservoirs in the hills above. The house at the bottom of the locks was once the Boatman Inn.

Reservoirs
Woodall Pond and Killamarsh Pond fed water into the top end of Norwood Locks. Their renewed use is being investigated as part of the canal's restoration.

Norwood Colliery Staithe
The stone-built wharf can be seen, just to the south of Bridge 29, where coal was loaded onto the boats. The colliery has long since disappeared.

Belk Lane Lock (No. 6)
Now in a private garden, the lock is just recognisable from the road bridge, infilled and used as a rockery and pond.

Killamarsh
Between Killamarsh and Spinkhill is the longest new cut caused by the construction of the railway in 1890–91. Landowner Ken Swain has restored nearly half a mile of the new cut for use as a fishery. The earthworks of the old canal route are visible, but run through private property. The railway is now a footpath. A detailed map of the route through the village is on page 33.

Spinkhill
Between Spinkhill and Renishaw the towpath skirts the boundary of the ironworks, and the canal has been buried by foundry waste.

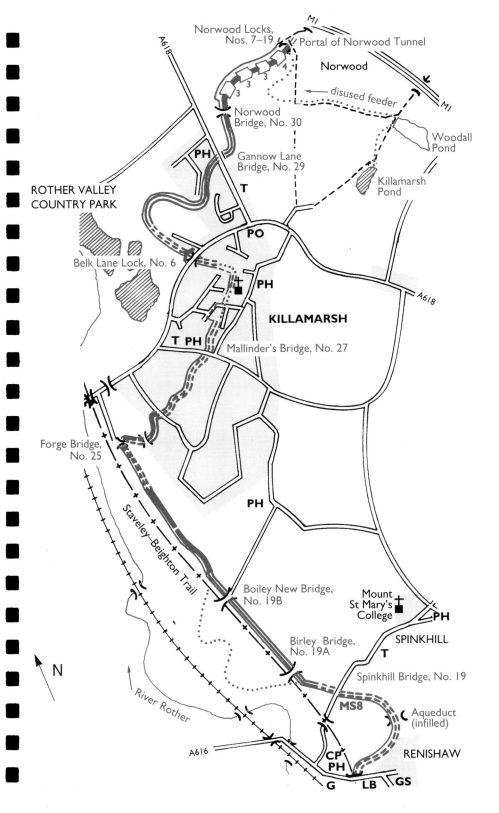

Killamarsh c. 1920, immediately north of Mallinder's Bridge (No. 27)

The ironworks north of Bridge 18 at Renishaw (now demolished)

The former Boatman Inn at the foot of Norwood Locks

Canal Society volunteers erecting a 'Cuckoo Way' towpath sign at Killamarsh

Killamarsh

Despite strenuous protests, the canal was built over in the 1970s. 'Cuckoo Way' signs have been erected to guide towpath walkers. At Bridge Street there is a wharf and a warehouse. Various alternative routes for a restored canal are being investigated.

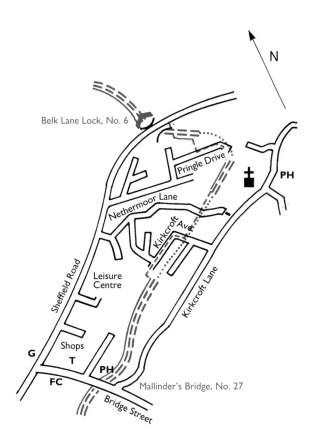

Map 4: *Kiveton Park*

4.25 miles (OS Pathfinder, Sheet 744)

General Area
The area is very pleasant and quiet, with wooded and open countryside. The canal follows the contours along the hillside. There is a good towpath.

Summit Pound
This is the name given to the four miles between Thorpe Locks and Norwood, where the canal is at its highest above sea level. The area is rich in limestone: old overgrown lime kilns and quarries can be seen along here.

There is a wooden bridge over an overflow section: this controls the canal's water level by allowing any excess to run into a local stream.

Dog Kennel Bridge
The name has been in use for over two centuries and may refer to the estate kennels of the Duke of Leeds, whose Kiveton Park main residence was nearby. This is a 'turnover' bridge where the towpath changes sides.

Stone for the Houses of Parliament
There was a wharf here, and in the 1840s it was busy with many loads of stone carted two miles from the Duke of Leeds's quarries in North Anston. The stone was loaded onto boats at Dog Kennels, taken to West Stockwith, transhipped into Trent sloops, and taken down the coast and up the Thames to Westminster — where it was used to build the Houses of Parliament. The original buildings were destroyed by fire in 1834 and the whole country was scoured for the best stone available to construct the building that we know today. One of the reasons North Anston was chosen was that transport costs were low, water transport being available from Kiveton Park to Westminster.

Harthill Feeder
This is the canal's main water supply from the reservoirs. There are walks around Harthill reservoir; details are on page 38.

Norwood Tunnel
The bricked-up eastern portal is visible here. On the bank to the right, when facing the entrance, the cellars of the house built for John Varley and his family can be found (Varley was the resident engineer who built the canal). It was also the company office for taking tolls as the boats passed in and out of the tunnel.

Norwood was a tremendous feat of 18th-century engineering, and is 2,893 yards long. It is brick-lined and straight, and took almost four years to complete. Shafts were sunk along its line, and the navvies were lowered down to work in both directions from the bottom of each shaft. When the sections were joined, it became, for a time, the longest canal tunnel in the country. The bricks were made in kilns along the top of the tunnel, and lowered down the shafts. We know of two navvies killed in the tunnel, but there may have been others.

There is no towpath; the boat-horses were led over the top of the tunnel, and the boats were 'legged' through by two of the crew who lay on their backs and 'walked' along the tunnel walls. Not a pleasant job.

Subsidence from the coal measures in the hillside plagued the tunnel almost as soon as it was finished. Repairs continued to undermine company profits until the expense could no longer be justified. On the 18th of October 1907 the roof collapsed, near Hard Lane, and was not repaired. Since then the Derbyshire end of the canal has been isolated.

Walking over the Tunnel
This is possible, but it does pass through the spoil area of Kiveton Park Colliery. It can be very bad after wet weather. There is a subway under the M1.

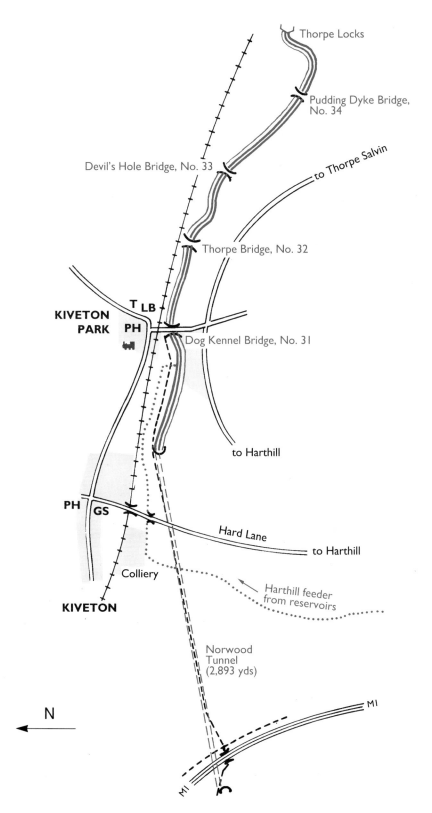

Thorpe Locks

Pudding Dyke Bridge, No. 34

Devil's Hole Bridge, No. 33

to Thorpe Salvin

Thorpe Bridge, No. 32

T LB

KIVETON PARK

PH

Dog Kennel Bridge, No. 31

to Harthill

PH GS

Hard Lane

to Harthill

Colliery

Harthill feeder from reservoirs

KIVETON

Norwood Tunnel (2,893 yds)

M1

M1

N

KIVETON PARK HOLDINGS LTD

KIVETON PARK   SHEFFIELD   S31 8NQ   TEL: 0909 770252

KIVETON PARK STEEL & WIRE WORKS LTD

Manufacturers of bright steel bars and wire in a full range of carbon and alloy specifications:

- *Bars 3mm to 76mm*
- *Coils 3mm to 38mm*
- *Fully MOD approved UK and International*

Kiveton Park   Sheffield S31 8NQ   Tel: 0909 770252   Fax: 0909 772949

BARMOND INTERNATIONAL LTD

Stockholders and merchants of steel products, specialising in flats and sections.

- *Precision cold-rolled steel strip*
- *Hot-rolled special shapes*
- *Cold-rolled flats and special shapes*

Park House   Kiveton Park   Sheffield S31 8NP   Tel: 0909 772101   Fax: 0909 515014

GREAVES OF SHEFFIELD LTD

Manufacturers of fine cabinets and cases for:

- *Cutlery and silverware*
- *Instruments and audio*
- *Precision woodwork and display*

Exchange Works   Sidney St   Sheffield S1 3QF   Tel: 0742 755302   Fax: 0742 768408

K.P.H. INDUSTRIAL SERVICES LTD

High-quality industrial services, provided by a versatile team of experienced engineers, covering:

- *Plant maintenance, refurbishment and installation*
- *Mechanical, electrical and hydraulic work*
- *Welding and steel fabrication, general machining*

Kiveton Park   Sheffield S31 8NQ   Tel: 0909 770252   Fax: 0909 772949

Harthill village

Harthill Village and Reservoirs

Often-forgotten features of canals are the reservoirs that supply much of the water. The reservoirs for the Chesterfield Canal are high on the ridge through which Norwood Tunnel passes. Harthill and Pebley Reservoirs are still in use and are maintained by British Waterways. The water from here flows down to the canal near Kiveton Park (see Map 4).

Harthill Reservoir has been enlarged over the years. Originally three separate areas of water, it has now merged into one. The two old dams have now been breached, and footbridges have been built where the dams used to be. The reservoir is used by Worksop & District Anglers and Rotherham sailing club, and it has footpaths around it. Eventually the paths will reach further up the valley to Pebley Reservoir.

Road Access

Carver Way (see map) is narrow — only one car's width — and looks like a footpath.

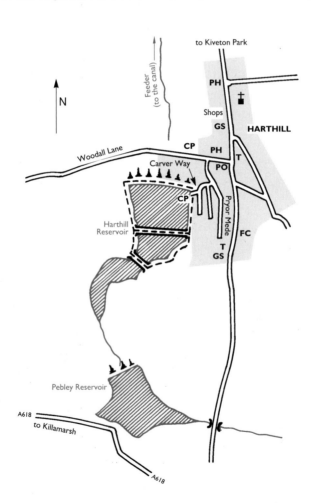

Circular Walk

● It is recommended that the appropriate OS map is used when following walks in this guide.

Lindrick Dale — Brancliffe Canal Feeder — Turnerwood — Canal — Thorpe Locks — Lindrick Dale

Three miles. Maps 4 and 5. OS Pathfinder, Sheet 744. Road access via the A57, two miles east of Anston, opposite Lindrick Hill Farm (grid ref. 539828). Best to park on the hard shoulder of the A57.

Take care. This walk crosses Lindrick Golf Course — please be aware of flying golf balls — and it is thoughtful to stand still and be quiet if a player is about to make a shot. The walk also crosses a railway line, but it is at designated public points.

Walk down the narrow road to the bottom of Lindrick Dale, where there are many fine gardens and a stream. At the end of the surfaced road, bear left, and then immediately left again onto a path uphill. Look for a sign saying 'Lindrick Golf Club'; go ahead past the sign and ahead along the edge of the golf course (note the yellow waymarks).

Follow the path through the woods; go straight across the fairway, across a second fairway, and right at the path T-junction. Cross the bridge over the infant River Ryton. Cross the Brancliffe feeder of the canal and go uphill into woods. Go through the woods, come out into a field, and cross this on a well-made path. The valley crossing the area ahead is the valley of the canal.

Go through the gate to Brancliffe Grange, right at the path junction and over a stile. Take the path across a field to another stile, meet the canal feeder and follow the path with the canal feeder on your left. Go over a stile, cross the railway and keep straight on towards Turnerwood on the canal.

Turn right onto the towpath, and follow this as you go past Thorpe Locks. At the next bridge — marked '1835' on the keystone — turn right off the towpath onto a public footpath over a grassy field. Go over a stile, cross the railway and then cross a field. Turn left onto a track, and go under a railway bridge.

Bear left at the path junction and then back to the bottom of Lindrick Dale. Bear left back to the A57.

Lindrick Dale — on the left the River Ryton, on the right the Brancliffe Feeder taking water to the canal at Turnerwood

Map 5: *Shireoaks*

3.5 miles (OS Pathfinder, Sheets 744 and 762)

General Area
Between Worksop and Shireoaks the canal skirts light industrial areas. From Shireoaks to the top of Thorpe Locks is through very pleasant, remote, quiet countryside. There is a good towpath.

Sandhill Lake
This is a flooded sand-quarry used for watersports and fishing.

Morse Lock (No. 49)
This lock is currently the head of the navigable part of the canal. Restoration and maintenance is being discussed by the Canal Society, local authorities and British Waterways. It was once known as 'Mossy Lock'.

Lady Lee Arm
Now infilled, it was built in the 1780s to take boats to the Lady Lee stone quarry. Its towpath can still be followed and is a public footpath. The remains of a small dock can be seen in the wooded section at the end; the quarry is now a small nature reserve.

Deep Lock (No. 47)
This lock lifted or dropped boats 10 feet instead of the average 4–6 feet of most of the canal's other locks. In the 1930s–40s it tended to be narrower at the bottom than others. Every working boatman knew his boat would jam inside the lock unless he was very careful.

Shireoaks Colliery Basin
The basin was built so that boats could be loaded with coal, down chutes from the bank. From 1908 to the 1940s this was usually the furthest point the working boats would visit; there were few cargoes beyond after Norwood Tunnel had closed.

Ryton Aqueduct
A three-arch aqueduct over the river, it also marks the Yorkshire–Nottinghamshire border.

Turnerwood Locks (Nos. 35–41)
There are seven single locks here. Between numbers 39 and 40, on the far bank, an arm of the canal used to take boats to a now disused stone quarry. The stone was used to build these and other locks.

Brancliffe Feeder
The Brancliffe Feeder empties water from the River Ryton into the canal between locks 38 and 39. Feeders are small canals in their own right — precisely surveyed to supply water at a steady rate, and usually with control points at each end. The circular walk on page 39 includes the course of this feeder.

Turnerwood
An attractive and secluded hamlet of cottages, Turnerwood was mainly built for the workers of the now disused nearby quarry, stone from which was carried on the canal.

Thorpe Locks (Nos. 20–34)
A tremendous early engineering achievement when built in 1773, this flight was the steepest in Britain. There are 15 locks in just over half a mile, including two treble and two double staircases (see page 7). The locks used to be a local tourist attraction known as the 'Giant's Staircase'.

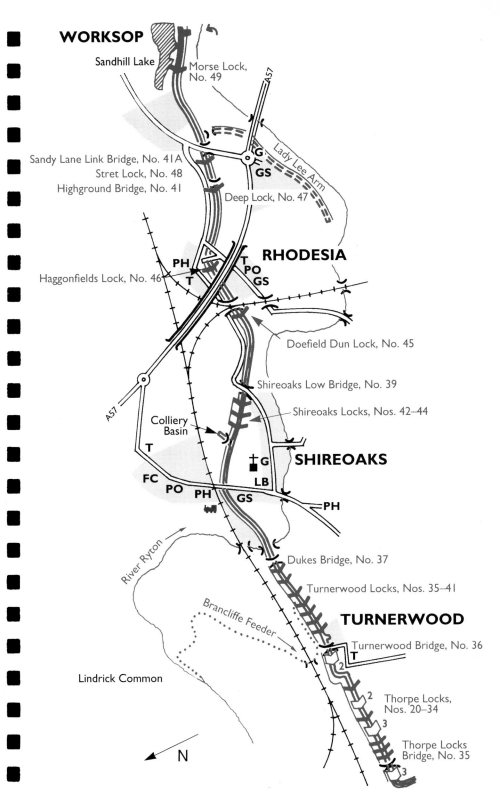

WORKSOP

Sandhill Lake

Morse Lock, No. 49

A57

Sandy Lane Link Bridge, No. 41A
Stret Lock, No. 48
Highground Bridge, No. 41

Lady Lee Arm

G
GS

Deep Lock, No. 47

PH

RHODESIA

T
PO
GS

T

Haggonfields Lock, No. 46

Doefield Dun Lock, No. 45

A57

Shireoaks Low Bridge, No. 39

Colliery Basin

Shireoaks Locks, Nos. 42–44

T

†G

SHIREOAKS

FC
PO   PH   GS   LB

PH

River Ryton

Dukes Bridge, No. 37

Turnerwood Locks, Nos. 35–41

Brancliffe Feeder

TURNERWOOD

Turnerwood Bridge, No. 36

T

2

Lindrick Common

2

Thorpe Locks, Nos. 20–34

3

Thorpe Locks Bridge, No. 35

3

← N

Crane base

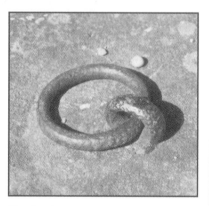

Mooring ring

Rope marks (see page 7) on Highground Bridge (No. 41), Worksop

Frozen Turnerwood

The culvert at Rhodesia, a typical restoration problem

Map 6: *Worksop*

3.5 miles (OS Pathfinder, Sheets 762 and 763)

Navigation
British Waterways moorings are situated before Town Lock. The Wharf complex by the straddle warehouse has water, and disposal points. One of the bottom gates of Town Lock is under the road bridge and awkward to open. A turning point for 70ft craft is a few hundred yards before the derelict Morse Lock. A head of navigation plaque register is held at the Canal Tavern; details are available from Ken Clark (telephone number on page 8). There is a launderette at 49 Gateford Road, just up from Town Lock, and a children's play area in the park, opposite the Priory Church. There is easy access to shopping, banks, etc.

General Area
Between Osberton and Manton the canal passes through wooded and open countryside. West of Manton the outskirts of Worksop are evident, although pleasant. There is a good towpath, but see the note below about passage past The Wharf and Town Lock.

Osberton Hall
The towpath changes sides past the hall — the 1771 owner had it written into the canal's Act of Parliament that the towpath must be on the opposite side to his house. Scofton is the village of the Osberton estate. The church (1833) has a stained-glass window with the arms of the Foljambe family from Plantagenet times.

Canal Feeder
This feeder carries water from the River Ryton to the canal. It has been formed into a feature of the town park (Memorial Avenue) and may be followed on foot from the Ryton to near Bracebridge Lock.

Bracebridge Pumping Station
The pumping station is the building with the tall chimney, now disused. It was built in 1881 as part of the town's sewage disposal system. It had a steam-driven beam engine, fired by coal brought by boat from Shireoaks Colliery.

Bracebridge Lock (No. 51)
The house by the side used to be the lock-keeper's cottage, now privately owned. Below the bridge was a stable for canal horses, and row-boats could be hired on the opposite bank.

Straddle Warehouse
Built over the canal, the warehouse was once owned by Pickford's. Overhead is the trapdoor where goods were hoisted and lowered to waiting boats; the winding gear is still on the top floor. It was opened as 'The Wharf' (restaurants) in 1994.

Towpath
To bypass the gate by Town Lock and The Wharf (eastwards), go into the canal-side car park, alongside Wilkinson's store, cross the main road, and go down the road with the high stone wall. To bypass westwards, take the road around The Wharf complex, cross the main road, and take the gap in the shops, almost opposite, into the canal-side car park.

Town Lock (No. 50)
A commemorative stone marks the 1977 bicentenary of the canal.

Above Town Lock
There used to be a basin off the canal, which is now a car park. It was lined with warehouses and maltings — boats chiefly carried coal in and malt out. The entrance is marked by a black post in the towpath.

Worksop (Town)
Worksop is a market town, known as the 'Gateway to the Dukeries' because of the many great estates in the area. The Priory Church, 12–14th century, has the only gatehouse in England with a wayside shrine and chapel. Entrance times are available from Tourist Information (page 8), as are 'Town Trail' walking and cycling leaflets, and bus and accommodation details. Clumber Park ('Sherwood Forester' bus from Worksop in summer) is five miles south-east with a National Trust park of 3,800 acres, and an 80-acre lake. Bicycle hire is available and there is a restaurant and a shop. These were once the grounds of the home of the Duke of Newcastle, a major shareholder in the canal company.

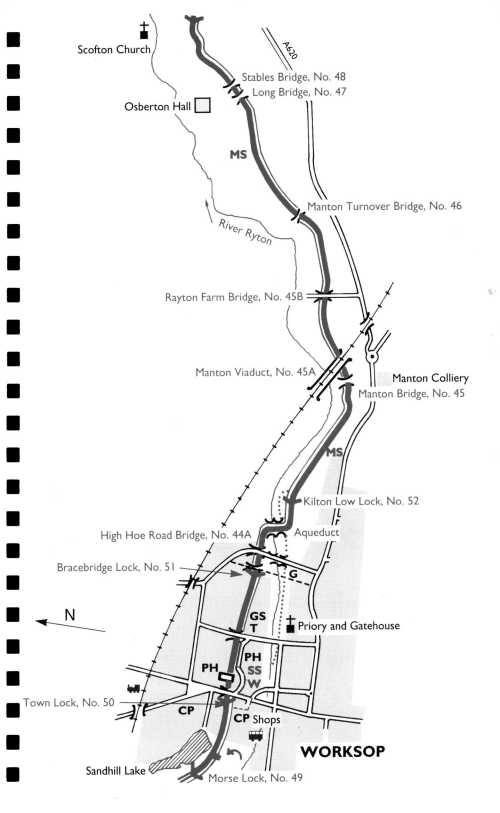

Scofton Church

Osberton Hall

Stables Bridge, No. 48
Long Bridge, No. 47

A620

MS

Manton Turnover Bridge, No. 46

River Ryton

Rayton Farm Bridge, No. 45B

Manton Viaduct, No. 45A

Manton Colliery

Manton Bridge, No. 45

MS

Kilton Low Lock, No. 52

High Hoe Road Bridge, No. 44A

Aqueduct

Bracebridge Lock, No. 51

G

GS
T

Priory and Gatehouse

N

PH
SS
W

PH

PH

Town Lock, No. 50

CP

CP Shops

WORKSOP

Sandhill Lake

Morse Lock, No. 49

J. Sainsbury, grocer.
Part of the local community.

We are pleased to support the
Canal Restoration

Worksop, below Morse Lock (No. 49)

The old straddle-warehouse, Worksop, now The Wharf restaurant

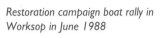

Restoration campaign boat rally in Worksop in June 1988

Bracebridge Lock, Worksop (No. 51)

Bridge No. 44 at Bracebridge Lock, Worksop

Map 7: *Ranby*

4.75 miles (OS Pathfinder, Sheet 745)

Navigation
The pub at Ranby has good moorings for customers alongside its beer garden, and also a barbecue site. Near the A1 bridge is a 70ft turning point. Above Osberton Lock there are a few Retford & Worksop Boat Club moorings on the non-towpath side. British Waterways facilities are available at Forest, and include a shower block, as well as short- and long-term moorings.

General Area
There is a good towpath. The countryside is quiet with few buildings, marred only for a short while by traffic noise from the A1 near Ranby.

Forest Locks (Nos. 54–57)
These were so called because the area was part of Sherwood Forest when the locks were built. 'Charlie's Lock' is named after a British Waterways employee who used to live in the cottage.

Barnby Wharf
Barnby Wharf can be found by the bridge, and is now used as a car park. The road over the bridge is a Roman route which formed part of the original Great North Road. That was until the citizens of Retford had the official route diverted through their town to gain passing trade. A mile to the north is Barnby Moor and the old posting house, 'Ye Olde Bell Hotel',

which rose to prominence when stagecoaches ran between London and York.

Kingfishers
Near Greenmile Bridge the canal passes through a wooded sandstone cutting, and this is a good area to look for kingfishers.

North of Ranby
There is a row of cottages on the towpath side, with doors facing the canal. The one with a doorway on the first floor used to be a malthouse.

Ranby
Ranby is a small rambling village which still manages to retain its charm, despite the A1. There are good bus links to Retford and Worksop and there is a timetable on the bus shelter.

Ranby Bends
The canal confirms its history near Ranby: the contour-hugging bends are typical of the early canals built by the famous engineer, James Brindley. This was always the most difficult length for the boatmen and their horses. The bends meant that the tow-rope between a horse and a boat reached some unusual angles, and a lack of concentration sometimes resulted in the boat running aground or the horse ending up in the canal.

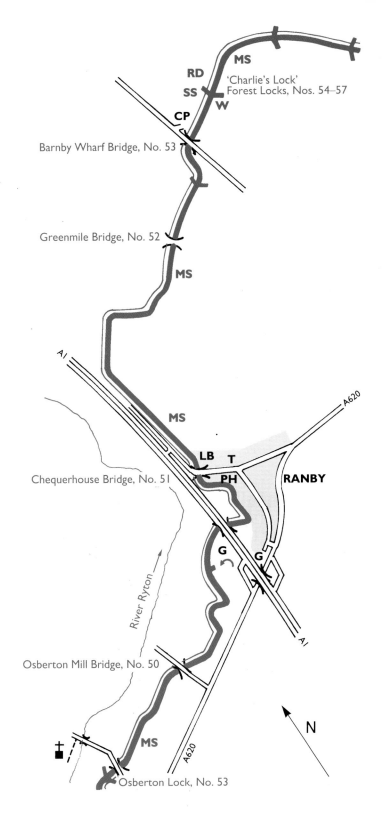

MS

RD

'Charlie's Lock'
Forest Locks, Nos. 54–57

SS

W

CP

Barnby Wharf Bridge, No. 53

Greenmile Bridge, No. 52

MS

A1

MS

LB   T

Chequerhouse Bridge, No. 51

PH

RANBY

A620

G   G

River Ryton

A1

Osberton Mill Bridge, No. 50

A620

MS

N

Osberton Lock, No. 53

British Waterways moorings at 'Charlie's Lock' (No. 55)

Retford basin, below Town Lock (No. 59)

Retford, near Inkerman Footbridge

Grove Mill, Retford — now a snooker club

Map 8: *Retford*

3.5 miles (OS Pathfinder, Sheet 745)

Navigation
All the locks above here are narrow. There are two turning points: one by Grove Mill Bridge, the other above West Retford Lock. Moorings above and below Town Lock give good access to the town and shops. The small basin below Town Lock is the headquarters of Retford Mariners' Boat Club, where limited moorings may be available by prior arrangement. There is a slipway for which a small charge is made. The top gate of Town Lock carries a public footpath over the canal — please try to delay people as little as possible.

General Area
There is a good towpath. The route through Retford is very pleasant — often tree-lined — and overlooks King's Park. It also has many historical features.

The Hop Pole
By Welham Bridge, the name of this pub is a reminder of the acres of hops that were grown in this area in the 18th century. The canal ruined this trade by bringing in hops from Kent that made a beer that was less bitter-tasting.

They Pulled the Plug Out
In the summer of 1978, near Grove Mill, a British Waterways dredging gang found an old chain on the canal bed. They pulled it up, an unknown plug came out, and the canal between the encompassing locks drained into the river! This received wide newspaper coverage, reaching as far as Dublin, Jersey and Scotland. Even Lloyd's Shipping List recorded it.

Grove Mill
This is a large canal-side building, now a pub and snooker club. It was originally a maltings, and later converted to a flour mill. Its sign shows a Mississippi Riverboat on the canal!

Packet Inn
Situated by Grove Mill Bridge, this was the terminus for the weekly packet boat from Clayworth that brought villagers and their goods to town on market day.

Canal Feeder
A few yards from Grove Mill Bridge a gap can be seen in the row of gardens on the non-towpath side, opposite the start of the open grassy area by the towpath. This was where a two-mile long feeder channel brought water from the River Idle. Built at the same time as the canal, the extra water was needed to supply the wide locks between here and West Stockwith (see below: 'Aqueducts').

Carolgate Bridge
It has been enlarged many times, as it used to carry the Great North Road into town. However, the brickwork of the original can still be seen underneath.

Town Lock (No. 59)
This is a narrow lock, as are all the others between here and Chesterfield. The narrowboats of the canal system are designed to fit into such locks: the boats are 6 feet 10 inches wide, the locks 7 feet.

Above Town Lock
There is a warehouse that was used for goods carried on the canal. The remains of the base of a crane used to hoist cargoes can also be seen.

Aqueducts
The canal skirts King's Park and passes over three aqueducts: two small single-arch types, and a larger three-arch construction over the River Idle. By this stands a pump to transfer water from the river to the canal; this replaced the original feeder from the Idle (see above).

Lady Bridge
Good examples of the grooves caused by the tow-ropes of the working boats can be seen here (see page 7).

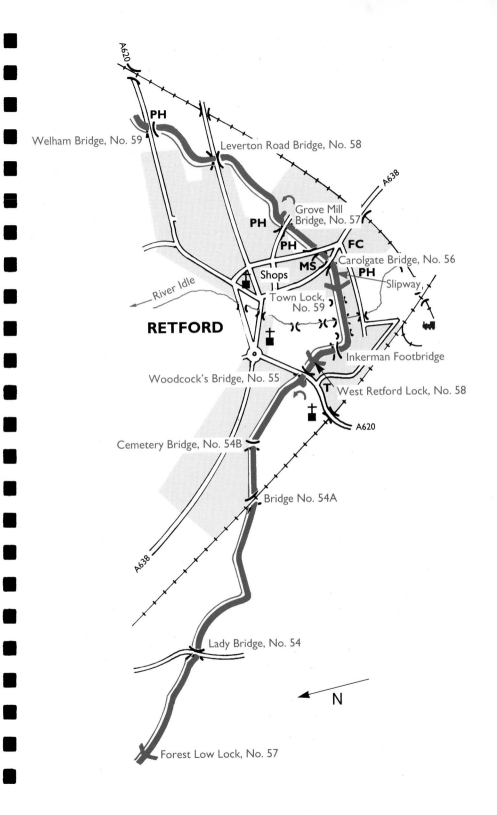

Welham Bridge, No. 59

PH

Leverton Road Bridge, No. 58

A620

A638

Grove Mill
Bridge, No. 57

PH

PH

FC

MS

Carolgate Bridge, No. 56

Shops

PH

Slipway

River Idle

Town Lock,
No. 59

RETFORD

Inkerman Footbridge

Woodcock's Bridge, No. 55

T

West Retford Lock, No. 58

A620

Cemetery Bridge, No. 54B

Bridge No. 54A

A638

Lady Bridge, No. 54

N

Forest Low Lock, No. 57

Retford

One of England's oldest boroughs, the town prospered because of its position on the Great North Road (constructed in 1766), the building of the canal (1777) and of the railway (1849). There is a busy market in the Square on Thursdays and Saturdays.

In the Market Square, in front of the **Town Hall**, is the **Broad Stone**. It used to stand several hundred yards away, and during the plague years the country folk would not venture nearer to market than this. The hollow was filled with vinegar into which the townspeople put their coins to pay for the food supplied by the villagers.

The church of **St Swithin's**, largely rebuilt in 1658, is floodlit at night. In front stands a cannon which was captured at Sebastopol in 1858 during the Crimean War. In World War II it was threatened with being melted down for the war effort, but it was saved when a Retford solicitor bought it and hid it.

The **Crown Inn** (Halifax Building Society) was the scene of many meetings of the canal proprietors during the 1770s, and of a political riot in 1774, which the canal navvies helped to quell before troops arrived. The canal engineer James Brindley addressed meetings here and at the **White Hart**.

King's Park has pleasant walks, including the canal and the River Idle. The river is the ancient boundary between East and West Retford, and an ancient ford here may have given the town its name: 'Red-ford', from the red mud that was churned up.

The **Tourist Information Office** and **Bassetlaw Museum** are in Amcott House on Grove Street.

Boaters' Facts

The shops in Carolgate and the Market Square are easily accessible from the canal, and there is a good selection of pubs, restaurants and takeaways. There is a fish and chip shop near Town Lock on Thrumpton Lane. There is no convenient launderette, but there is one in Worksop.

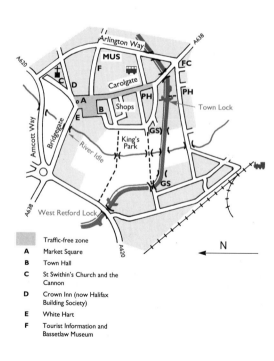

A	Market Square
B	Town Hall
C	St Swithin's Church and the Cannon
D	Crown Inn (now Halifax Building Society)
E	White Hart
F	Tourist Information and Bassetlaw Museum

Traffic-free zone

Circular Walks

- It is recommended that the appropriate OS map is used when following these walks.

Clarborough — Hayton — Clarborough

2.5 miles. Map 9. OS Pathfinder, Sheet 745. Road access via the B1403 at Clarborough, and via Smeath Lane.

From Bridge 62 (the Gate Inn), follow the road towards Clarborough. Cross the main road and take the road uphill (marked 'A620 Gainsborough'). Before reaching the top of the hill, turn left onto a path (signed 'bridleway').

The path has views and hedges to the left and arable fields to the right. Keep straight on at the path junctions until after the path becomes better surfaced.

At the next junction turn left down a surfaced path/road and bear left at the bottom — the Boat Inn at Bridge 66 can now be seen. Cross the canal, turn left along the towpath — Bridge 63 has rope marks — and follow the towpath back to Bridge 62.

Misterton — River Idle — West Stockwith — River Trent — Canal — Misterton

Three miles. Map 12. OS Pathfinder, Sheet 728. Road access via the A161 where it crosses the canal at Misterton.

From the Misterton Bottom Lock (the Packet Inn), go north along Soss Lane, under the railway, past Orchard Close and continue to the bank of the River Idle. (The building with two tall chimneys is Misterton Soss, an old pumping station used to raise water from the Mother Drain up into the Idle. It was built between 1828 and 1839.)

Turn right along the Idle and follow it to West Stockwith. The first barrier seen across the Idle is a pumping station used to control water levels to prevent flooding further upriver. The near side has a gate that can be lifted to allow boat access.

The second barrier is a vertical flood control gate which is raised at low tide to allow the Idle to flow into the Trent, and closed at other times to keep the Trent out.

At West Stockwith turn right along the main road. At the end of the green piling, go through the white gate and climb the steps to the bank of the Trent. Go along the bank to West Stockwith canal basin, under the bridge at the corner of the basin, and follow the towpath back to Misterton.

Misterton Soss on the River Idle

Map 9: *Clarborough*

2.5 miles (OS Pathfinder, Sheet 745)

Navigation
The nine-mile pound ends at Whitsunday Pie Lock. Care should be taken navigating the sharp bend at Clarborough Top Bridge. Otherwise this is a straightforward section. The Boat Inn at Hayton and The Gate at Clarborough have moorings for customers.

General Area
There is a good towpath. The countryside is open farmland, with the canal keeping to one contour by hugging the side of a small ridge. By keeping level this way, the original engineers built nine miles without a lock.

Hayton
A quiet farming village with a succession of old farms and attractive canal bridges. By Townend Bridge the Boat Inn has a garden, a restaurant, and a children's play area.

Church Bridge
The nearby St Peter's Church dates from the 12th century, the oldest part being the north wall of the nave. It has original box pews.

Clarborough
The car park at the Gate Inn used to be a wharf with a weighbridge for goods being delivered by canal. There is a children's playground. The King's Arms in the village has a grassed playground at the rear.

Bonemill Bridge
The building on the non-towpath side was where bones brought by boat were crushed to make fertilisers.

Welham
The name comes from the once-renowned well that is still below the floor of a house on Bonemill Lane. The well used to be visited by people seeking a cure for rheumatism because the beautifully clear water contains magnesium and gypsum.

Whitsunday Pie Lock (No. 60)
A wide lock, as are all the others between here and West Stockwith, it is capable of taking two narrowboats side by side. Because of its unusual name, it is the most famous lock on the canal. The popular reason for the name is that a farmer's wife baked a huge pie to celebrate the opening of the lock at Whitsunday. Indeed this event is commemorated by the Retford & Worksop Boat Club at an annual boat-gathering, when a pie is served on the lockside. However, and perhaps unfortunately, recent research has proved that the name existed before the lock was constructed and probably has mundane roots as a field name: the first part relating to a tenancy changing at Whitsun, the second part derived from the old word 'pightle', meaning a small enclosure or croft.

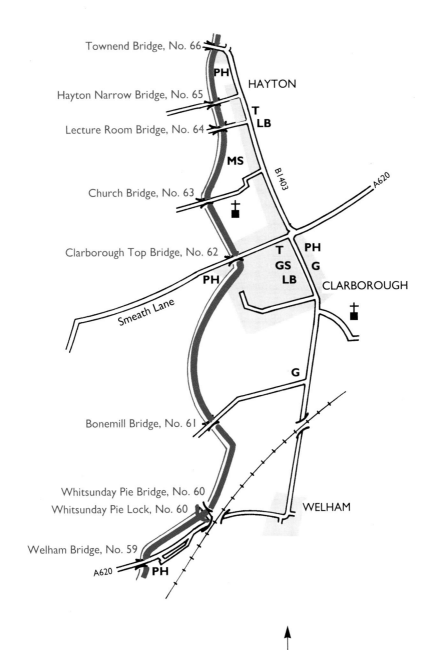

Townend Bridge, No. 66

PH

HAYTON

Hayton Narrow Bridge, No. 65

T
LB

Lecture Room Bridge, No. 64

MS

B1403

A620

Church Bridge, No. 63

✝

Clarborough Top Bridge, No. 62

T
GS
LB

PH
G

PH

CLARBOROUGH

✝

Smeath Lane

G

Bonemill Bridge, No. 61

Whitsunday Pie Bridge, No. 60
Whitsunday Pie Lock, No. 60

WELHAM

Welham Bridge, No. 59

A620

PH

N

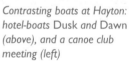

*Contrasting boats at Hayton:
hotel-boats* Dusk *and* Dawn
*(above), and a canoe club
meeting (left)*

Clayworth, 1959. The pub is now the HQ of the Retford & Worksop Boat Club.

A boulder set into the wall of Clayworth churchyard. One story is that it was found by the navvies building the canal in the 1770s — and placed in the wall in memory of a workmate killed on the project.

Map 10: *Clayworth*

3.5 miles (OS Pathfinder, Sheet 745)

Navigation
The turning point at Clayworth Bridge is really the apex of the bend; 70ft craft may find it difficult to turn here because of moored craft. Long-term or temporary moorings may be arranged with the Retford & Worksop Boat Club, a member of the Association of Waterways Cruising Clubs (telephone number on page 8). The British Waterways facilities are near the clubhouse. The post office is also a small general store.

General Area
There is a good towpath through quiet, open countryside. South of Clayworth it is remote, with views to the westward across many miles of flat carr-land.

Grey's Bridge
The large house on the road is Clayworth Manor, once the home of the Grey family after whom the bridge is named. The road crossing the canal here is the Roman route between Lincoln and Doncaster.

Otter's Bridge
The large building on the non-towpath side is the Elizabethan Royston Manor, dating from 1588. Until 1948 it was the home of the Otter family, and this bridge linked their lands across the canal.

Clayworth
The oldest part of Clayworth is near the church — here most of the buildings along the narrow street date from the 1700s. Although the canal skirts the village, its proximity has had an effect over the last two centuries. The wall around the 13th-century St Peter's Church has a large boulder set into it, on the corner. One of the many stories is that it was found by the navvies building the canal, and they asked for it to be put in the wall as a memorial to one of their mates who had been killed. Others say it is a meteorite.

The Brewer's Arms used to brew its own beer until supplies from town breweries were brought to the village by canal. Hops still grow wild in the hedgerows nearby.

Before piped supplies, the water from Clayworth wells was thought to be 'the elixir of life': it was pure, sparkling and ice cold, but it made such a terrible cup of tea that many villagers preferred to use water from the canal.

It was too far for the boat-horses to go to the village smithy, so they had their own smithy on the canal bank, now the post office.

Packet Boat
Every week a packet boat used to leave Clayworth to take villagers and their produce to Retford market. The goods were loaded late on Friday evening and the boat left at 6.30 on Saturday morning. It reached Retford at 8.30 and returned to Clayworth in the evening. This lasted until the 1920s when the proprietor purchased Clayworth's first bus.

Clayworth Bridge
Clayworth Bridge was built in the 1830s to replace the original wooden swing bridge. The colourful moored boats of the Retford & Worksop Boat Club stretch for many yards along the canal. The clubhouse used to be a canal pub, the White Hart, and there were overnight stables for the boat-horses.

Retford & Worksop Boat Club
In the 1960s the club played an important part in keeping the canal open. At that time the canal was barely navigable, and the founders of the RWBC organised weed-busting cruises to Worksop to prove it was used and should not be abandoned.

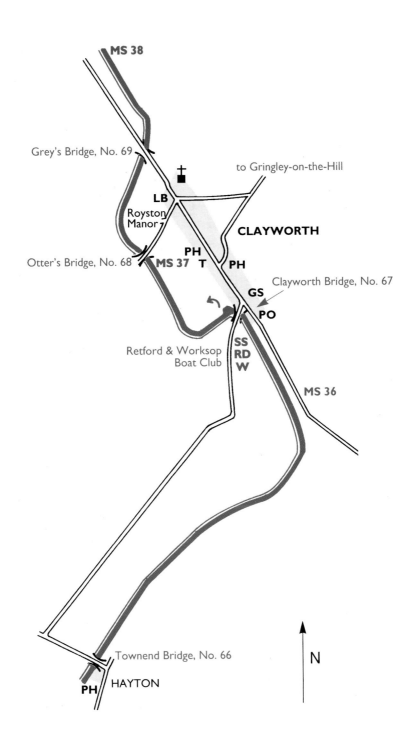

MS 38

Grey's Bridge, No. 69

to Gringley-on-the-Hill

LB

Royston
Manor

CLAYWORTH

Otter's Bridge, No. 68

MS 37

PH
T

PH

Clayworth Bridge, No. 67

GS

PO

Retford & Worksop
Boat Club

SS
RD
W

MS 36

Townend Bridge, No. 66

HAYTON

PH

N

The stable-block in Wiseton village

Picnic at Drakeholes

John Lower's boat, Madeley Wood, *leaving Shaw Lock (No. 62)*

The old brickworks near Shaw Lock (No. 62)

Map 11: *Drakeholes*

4.25 miles (OS Pathfinder, Sheet 728)

Navigation
There are good moorings above Shaw Lock. Gringley Top Lock is the start of a nine-mile pound. Drakeholes Tunnel is short (154 yards), and straight, with no towpath. At the southern end is a 90° left turn — please approach slowly. Shorter boats can turn here at the apex of the bend, but moored craft may be near. Immediately after the turn there is a slipway on the right, controlled by the Retford & Worksop Boat Club, which extends out under the waterline. At Wiseton Top Bridge approaching craft cannot be seen.

General Area
There is a good towpath through quiet countryside. Between Gringley Top Lock and Drakeholes there are good views across the flat carr-lands. If you can see two power stations, the nearest is Thorpe Marsh (14 miles), and the other is Drax (20 miles). Between Drakeholes and Wiseton the terrain is more wooded. The canal bends around the Wiseton Estate as there was an order to keep away from the hall when the canal was built.

Shaw Lock (No. 62)
The mark on the bridge keystone is the date of construction and the initials of the builder or landowner. In a nearby field can be seen the chimney of an old brickworks. Boats were loaded and unloaded just above the lock — they brought coal in and carried bricks out.

Gringley-on-the-Hill
Gringley is an old village, and a stiff uphill walk from the canal. Beacon Hill is at the end of High Street; access is through the white gate by the road. There are views of 20–30 miles in all directions: to the south, Lincoln Cathedral's triple towers are 20 miles away — some claim to have seen York Minster 40 miles to the north.

Drakeholes Tunnel
The towpath goes over the tunnel top; from the south it is over the road, and by the 'Give Way' sign. The horses were taken this way, while their boats were pushed through by the crew levering boat-poles on the tunnel sides.

Drakeholes
Drakeholes is popular with visitors to the canal and the Griff Inn. There used to be a busy wharf here: regular packet boats called; goods were loaded, unloaded and transhipped between road and canal; and stagecoaches

stopped. It was a convenient arrangement because the boats had to stop anyway to hitch and unhitch their horses because of the tunnel. The landlord of the pub (then called the White Swan) organised the wharf and the cargoes. Above the tunnel are two dilapidated gate lodges that mark the entrance to the old drive to Wiseton Hall, made redundant when the drive was re-aligned.

Man Face Bridge
This bridge is more ornate, with a weathered face on the keystones, because it carried the main drive to Wiseton Hall. Between Man Face Bridge and Taylor's Bridge, on the non-towpath side, is an overgrown ornamental garden. Flowering shrubs, palm trees and yuccas can still be seen among the foliage.

Wiseton Hall and Village
This is an estate village with the cottages named after trees or flowers. The present hall replaced the original in 1962 and is hidden behind high walls. The village was once the hub of a 3,800-acre estate. The stable block, with its clock tower, was built in 1899 for the racehorses of Sir Joseph Laycock. Yew Tree Cottage was the home of the hall's butler. From 1814 to 1863 the estate was owned by the Spencer ancestors of the Princess of Wales, and was the favourite residence of the 3rd Earl.

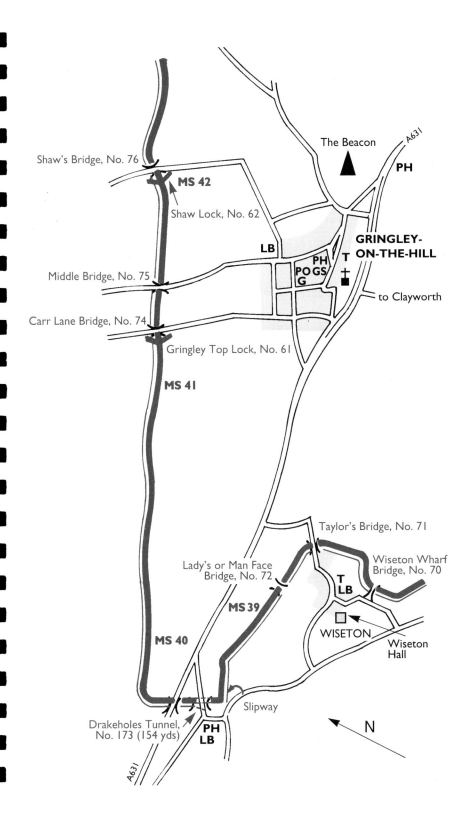

Shaw's Bridge, No. 76

MS 42

Shaw Lock, No. 62

The Beacon

A631

PH

**GRINGLEY-
ON-THE-HILL**

LB

**PH
PO GS
G**

T
✝
■

Middle Bridge, No. 75

to Clayworth

Carr Lane Bridge, No. 74

Gringley Top Lock, No. 61

MS 41

Taylor's Bridge, No. 71

Lady's or Man Face
Bridge, No. 72

Wiseton Wharf
Bridge, No. 70

**T
LB**

MS 39

□

MS 40

WISETON

Wiseton
Hall

Slipway

N

Drakeholes Tunnel,
No. 173 (154 yds)

**PH
LB**

A631

West Stockwith Lock. Yacht race competitors locking down to the River Trent.

Approaching Misterton Top Lock (No. 63)

Safe arrival from the River Trent — in West Stockwith Lock (No. 65)

Map 12: *West Stockwith*

3.75 miles (OS Pathfinder, Sheet 728)

Navigation
Manor Farm Bridge, narrow and low at the edges, restricts wide craft — details are on page 75. There is a turning point immediately before it. At Cooper's Bridge approaching craft cannot be seen.

General Area
There is a good towpath through pleasant, quiet countryside. By the Trent the area is remote: some say desolate, others tranquil. The canal skirts the edge of Misterton; elsewhere it is secluded and runs along the side of a ridge on the edge of the highly fertile Isle of Axholme.

River Trent
One of England's premier rivers, here it is tidal and often fast-flowing. Ships from Europe can be seen going to and from Gainsborough, as well as barges that go further upriver. River traffic depends on the tide.

West Stockwith Village
The village is situated a third of a mile from the canal basin, where the River Idle flows into the Trent. From the 14th century it was busy and prosperous because the River Idle was the old route for moving goods to the Trent. Goods were transhipped between the two rivers; the Trent was lined with warehouses and boat-building yards. Packet boats used to call on their way to Hull, and a ferry crossed to East Stockwith. The remaining signs of that age are the large houses near the Trent, built for the wealthy shipowners. The canal killed River Idle trade, and with it West Stockwith's prosperity.

River Idle
Like the Trent, it has flood banks to protect the low-lying land. It also has two large sluices: these keep out Trent tides and also pump and regulate water to drain the surrounding area. Page 57 has more details.

Packet Inn, Misterton
Early 19th-century packet boats called here: there was a passenger service to Retford every Wednesday and Saturday, and a service to Gainsborough via the Trent on Tuesday and Thursday. There was a daily goods service to Retford, Worksop, Chesterfield, Hull and Gainsborough.

Between Misterton Locks
On the far bank was the Albion Flour Mill. Built in 1840, it was one of the few powered by canal water, supplied via a small reservoir near the top lock. The boatmen used to stop at the mill to buy oats for their horses.

Misterton Bottom Lock
The by-wash goes under the road and flows back into the canal from under an old building below the lock.

Misterton
Misterton is a large village — agricultural, industrial and residential. The surrounding area used to be a large marsh until drained by the Dutch engineer Vermuyden in the 17th century. The canal brought prosperity: cottages and warehouses lined the road to Wharf Bridge.

Wharf Bridge (No. 81)
Has rope marks (see page 7), and an old rope post to protect the bridge.

Walkeringham Brickworks
This can be recognised by the tall chimneys near Smith's Bridge, and was once famous for high-quality bricks and pantiles. Coal from higher up the canal was delivered by boats, which were then reloaded with bricks for delivery. The lake behind the house is where the clay for the bricks was extracted.

Warp
When the brick trade ceased, warp was produced. At low tide on the Trent, silt was shovelled into canal boats and then brought to the old brickworks. There it was dried and sieved until it was so fine and soft it made a perfect polish for cleaning silver. This trade was responsible for the last commercial traffic on the canal in the late 1950s. Eventually dredgers and road transport took over until production of warp finished in 1981.

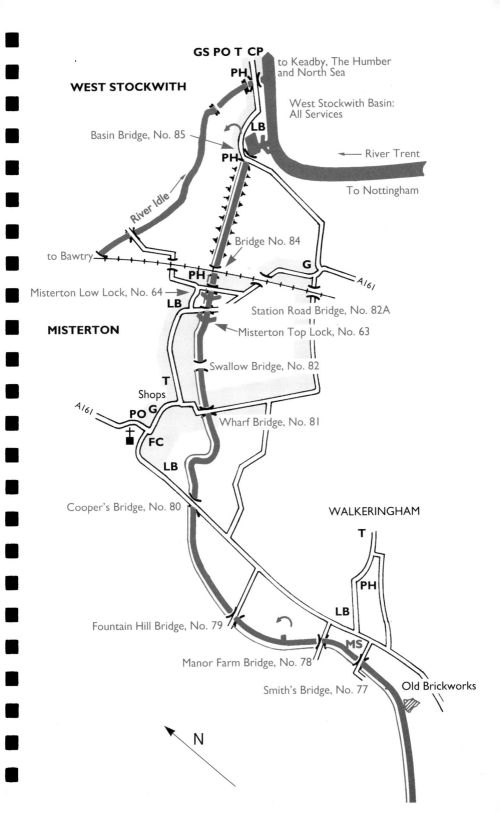

Shaw Lock (No. 62) with milestone 42 in the foreground

West Stockwith basin: the new moorings were installed in 1993

Dutch-gable houses by West Stockwith basin — a style traditional in the area since the 17th century when Dutch engineers drained the marshes

West Stockwith Basin

Navigation
The lock is *always* operated by the lock-keeper. His office is in the old warehouse, his house is on the opposite side. See page 77 for telephone number and hours of operation.

Many people visit the basin to look at the boats, and are very interested when the large lock into the Trent is in operation. *Locks can be dangerous places. Please do as the lock-keeper wishes. He is only thinking of your safety.*

Present
The building by the lock, containing the lock-keeper's office, is an old warehouse. Its date of construction, 1789, is marked high on the wall facing the river. It used to have a third floor, but this was removed when it became unsafe. The building at the side of the warehouse

used to be the stables for the canal boat-horses. The clubhouse of the West Stockwith Yacht Club used to be the offices of the agent responsible for organising cargoes and transport.

Past
Barges and keels from the Trent were brought into the basin for unloading. The inlet to the left when leaving the lock was where they moored, and goods could be craned direct into the warehouse. The canal boats were loaded and unloaded to the right of the lock. Many canal boats were built in the basin, on the side near the road. On the river bank, in front of the lock-keeper's house, is a winch which was used to pull the old engineless boats on the river towards the lock entrance.

Vessels on the River Trent at West Stockwith

Navigation of the Canal

The canal is navigable from West Stockwith to Worksop, a distance of 26 miles. However, restoration work is under way at the head of navigation and extra cruising miles may soon be available. There are also restored sections at Chesterfield for trailable boats.

Locks
The five locks from West Stockwith to Retford are wide, the remainder are narrow. All will accept 70ft craft.

Bridges
Although the locks to Retford are wide, some bridges on this section restrict use. The railway bridge at Misterton, just downstream of the Packet Inn, has 7 feet 9 inches headroom. The most restricted is Bridge 78 (Manor Farm) which has a towpath that prevents craft from passing centrally under the arch. It is not normally passable by cruisers wider and higher than the 7ft 6ins-beam Freeman 22s and 23s. Measurements by the Ripon Motor Boat Club show 6 feet 5 inches of height available 6 feet 3 inches from the edge of the channel. There is a turning point immediately before the bridge. The lowest is Bridge 77 (Smith's), available headroom under its flat span is 7 feet 3 inches.

Water Depth
This obviously changes, but 1992 echo-soundings by the Ripon Motor Boat Club show a channel generally in excess of 3 feet deep as far as the Retford & Worksop Boat Club moorings at Clayworth, but it reduces in a few places to 2 feet 6 inches. The canal is sometimes shallow near the edges, and a good-length gangplank may be needed.

Tunnels
Drakeholes Tunnel is 154 yards long, and wide, with no towpath. The disused 2,893-yard Norwood Tunnel near Killamarsh is a future restoration project.

Weed
This is a problem only at certain times of the year, usually late summer and autumn, although British Waterways are trying to combat it. The time, density and location differ each year as growth is dependent on the amount of sunshine and depth of water during the summer. However, it dies down each winter and there are seldom problems at that time, or in the spring and early summer.

Supplies
West Stockwith Basin is the only location on the canal for gas, diesel and pump-out.

Moorings
British Waterways has long-term moorings at West Stockwith, Forest Locks and Worksop.

Turning Points
At the current head of navigation, 70ft craft can turn above Town Lock, Worksop. Other points are at: Manor Farm Bridge (No. 78), Clayworth, Retford and Ranby. All are marked on the maps.

Slipways
The one at West Stockwith Basin is controlled by a British Waterways lock-keeper (see page 77 for the telephone number). Telephone numbers for the following are on page 8: Drakeholes (Retford & Worksop Boat Club); Retford Basin (Retford Mariners' Boat Club); Chesterfield (Derbyshire County Council, Ranger Service).

River Trent Navigation

The only access to the Chesterfield Canal for non-trailable boats is via the River Trent at West Stockwith. Here the Trent is tidal and carries large commercial vessels. However, do not allow these facts to deter you, to be safe you must respect the Trent, not fear it. Ask — and follow — the advice of the Stockwith lock-keeper. Also helpful is an item by John Lower in the July 1988 edition of *Waterways World*: 'Calculated Cruising: Trent Tideway Tips'.

Navigating the Trent

Before setting out, check your boat and its equipment and ensure you have adequate fuel. Boat-ropes should be at least 30 feet long to enable them to reach the locksides. Carry an anchor and cable (minimum 60 feet), free of obstructions and ready to drop. Many boat crews wear life jackets and this is strongly recommended, especially for children. Use the tide to help your journey, fighting it is a waste of fuel and time. River charts are recommended (see opposite page). Remember that large vessels need the deep channel: try to meet them on a straight section, move over to one side, and *stay* there. Do not dart about undecided.

They may use horn signals and will appreciate it if you know what they mean.

Keep a good lookout fore and aft and concentrate. The large vessels travel fast, but if you see them and move out of the way there should be no problems.

Aegre (Pronounced 'ā-ger').

The Aegre is a tidal bore which occasionally travels up the river from the Humber to Torksey or beyond. The National Rivers Authority issues a free annual timetable (see opposite page). The wave may be a few inches to 5 feet in height and it occurs at Flood. It usually needs a tide of over 8.5 metres at Hull, no flood water in the river, and no wind. However, if you cannot avoid it meet it head-on in the middle of the river.

West Stockwith Lock

See opposite for hours of operation. The bottom gates open direct from the Trent and are kept closed unless the keeper knows you are coming. If the lock is not ready, there is a good mooring wall on the upstream (Torksey) side of the lock with ladders, and the water here is almost current-free. If you have not entered Stockwith before, it is best to moor at the wall and ask the keeper's advice as the flow across the lock entrance can be tricky. *Always turn into the flow to approach the wall or the lock.*

The River Trent near Gainsborough

River Trent Navigation Facts

• *Telephone numbers: the digits in brackets to be omitted when dialling before 1st August 1994.*

Definition of Terms

Ebb Tide: when the river is running out towards the sea; lasts approximately ten hours.

Flood: when the tide stops ebbing and turns to come back in; it changes direction very quickly.

Flood Tide: when the tide is running in; lasts approximately 2½ hours; the flow is very fast.

High Water: the tide stops running in.

Slack Water: the tide is not going in or out; lasts approximately ten minutes. Then the *Ebb Tide* starts again for ten hours.

• To make life simpler, it is worth remembering that *Flood* at Stockwith is the same time as *High Water* at Hull, the point quoted in some tide tables. Times are GMT, so an hour must be added during British Summer Time.

Tide Tables and Aegre Schedule
National Rivers Authority, Corringham Road, Gainsborough DN21 1QH
Tel: 0(1)427 612205

Trent Charts
Trent Boating Association, 78 Old Retford Road, Sheffield S13 9RA

Trent Locks Telephones
West Stockwith	0(1)427 890204
Cromwell	0(1)636 821213
Torksey	0(1)428 771202
Keadby	0(1)724 782205

West Stockwith Lock
Maximum Size of Craft: 72ft × 17ft 6ins

Telephone: 0(1)427 890204

Radio Frequency: Calling channel 16; working channel 74. The radio is *not* constantly manned.

Operating hours: Only when the tide is over a certain height, generally from 2½ hours before High Water to 4½ hours after High Water. Low water levels may cause earlier closure. If these times will be before 8am or after 10pm, lock passage must be booked with the keeper 24 hours in advance, but is at his discretion.

Licences
The Trent here is controlled by Associated British Ports, but a standard canal licence does cover use of the river to reach the canal. If you only have a British Waterways river licence, a temporary haven licence is required to use the basin, or a short-stay canal licence. All are available from the West Stockwith lock-keeper.

Moorings
Temporary moorings can be arranged with the lock-keeper, but long stays should be booked prior to arrival.

Horn Signals
1 I am turning to starboard (right)
2 I am turning to port (left)
3 My engines are going in reverse

Notes

Index

Boat-building, c. 1920